AKALI BABA HANUMAN SINGH

A WARRIOR WHO FOUGHT A WAR AGAINST BRITISH AT THE AGE OF 90

ISHWAR SINGH

Copyright © Ishwar Singh
All Rights Reserved.

This book has been published with all efforts taken to make the material error-free after the consent of the author. However, the author and the publisher do not assume and hereby disclaim any liability to any party for any loss, damage, or disruption caused by errors or omissions, whether such errors or omissions result from negligence, accident, or any other cause.

While every effort has been made to avoid any mistake or omission, this publication is being sold on the condition and understanding that neither the author nor the publishers or printers would be liable in any manner to any person by reason of any mistake or omission in this publication or for any action taken or omitted to be taken or advice rendered or accepted on the basis of this work. For any defect in printing or binding the publishers will be liable only to replace the defective copy by another copy of this work then available.

I am dedicating this book to the unsung Heroes of the Sikh history.

Contents

Foreword

Ishwar Singh have more than ten years of experience in writing story books, sakhis of devotional saints and in research activities. He is a tremendous writer. He is doing excellent job by writing about **Akali Baba Hanuman Singh.** *He had shown very keen interest in the field of historical resources and other cultural issues.*

He is also a very excellent teacher and also having deep knowledge about the social science issues. I have always seen him working very hard for his various books. He just want to express about the Indian culture to our new generations in a simple and brief manner. I wish him all the very best for his new book.

Preface

This book is about the brief history of Akali Baba Hanuman Singh who had fought a war against Britishers at the age of 90 under very hard circumstances. The task behind to publish such content is to spread knowledge about the unsung heroes of the Sikh history among the new generation. In the schools, which are being organised by Sikh trusts, the students are just getting very limited knowledge about the Sikh warriors. Baba Banda Singh Bahadur, Baba Deep Singh, Hari Singh Nalua etc. are the common names on the tongues of the students but they don't know about the others. This is just an effort to spread this brief information among new generations.

Ishwar Singh

Acknowledgements

I'm eternally grateful to my father Pal Singh, who took in an extra mouth to feed when he didn't have to. He taught me discipline, tough love, manners, respect, and so much more that has helped me succeed in life. I truly have no idea where I'd be if he hadn't given me a roof over my head whom I desperately needed at that age.

I would like to thanks the Sikh Encyclopaedia, the Sikhiwiki Which is is a free, multilingual, open content encyclopaedia project about Sikhism.

To my father-in-law Narinder Singh for their moral support during the up and downs in my life. He taught me how to live positive even in the worst situations by sharing his personal experiances. He is the man who suggest me to write a book in your life because it will be your book by which you will be remembered in future.

To Dr. Davinder Singh, who never saw my age, my race, or my lack of formal education. He just saw a kid hungry to learn, hungry to grow, and hungry to succeed in teaching. He never stopped me; he only encouraged me.

Finally, to all those who have been a part of my getting there: Sukhbir Singh, Jarnail Singh, Beant Kaur, Devinder Kumar Sharma, Sumeet Kaur, Rinkpal Singh, Iqbal Singh and Manpreet Singh.

ONE

AKALI BABA HANUMAN SINGH

During the rule of Maharaja Ranjit Singh, there was a regiment whose name was Akal Regiment. The interesting fact about this regiment was that it was an idependent regiment and work according to their own strategy. Maharaja Ranjit Singh has himself given lots of respect to this regiment. Akal regiment was popularly known as the Budha Dal, a leading organisation of Sikh warriors.

Akali Baba Hanuman Singh Ji (1755-1845), the 7th leader of the Budha Dal, was born to Baba Garja Singh Ji and Mata Harnam Kaur Ji in November 1755, in the village of Naurang Singh Wala, near Zira in Firozpur district of Punjab. Baba Ji fought in many great battles under the leadership of Akaali Baba Naina Singh Ji and Akaali Baba Phula Singh Ji (the 5th and 6th Jathedars of Budha Dal).

After the Shaheedi of Akaali Phula Singh Ji at Naushera in 1823, Baba Hanuman Singh Ji became the leader of the Akaali Nihangs, as well as the Jathedar of Akaal Takht Sahib at the age of 68 years.

Akaali Baba Hanuman Singh Ji's tenure as Jathedar of the Sikh nation came as the Panth was experiencing a very critical time. In 1839 the Maharaja of the Punjab, Ranjit Singh died from stroke complications, his successors were murdered, the treacherous Dogra's sold out the Lahore Darbar to the British, and the British were planning on annexing the Punjab.

Maharani Jind Kaur, at that time the Empress of the Sikh kingdom of the Punjab, the most, trusted Sikh general Sardar Sham Singh Attarivala came to the holy city of Amritsar and approached Jathedar Hanuman Singh for assistance against the British.

Meeting at the Akaal Takht, Sham Singh said to Baba Hanuman Singh "Baba Ji, I wish to fight against the British, but have no army. I have no more then myself and my sons."

Baba Ji replied "Oh Singh Ji, who does this Akaali fauj belong to, if not to the Sikh nation."

During the battle of Sabraon, in 1846 Sardar Sham Singh Ji, Attarivala and many Sikh warriors received martyrdom fighting the British soldiers, inflicting huge losses to the invaders.

Baba Hanuman Singh Ji and the remaining Singhs went to camp out in the Sikh Princely state of Patiala. The King of Patiala, Maharaja Karam Singh (Captain Amrinder Singh, who is the former Chief Minister of Punjab belongs to the same dynasty i.e. Maharaja Karam Singh was the forefather of Captain Amrinder singh) upon receiving word that the knights of the Tenth Sikh Guru, were camped out in his state, out of fear of retribution for his support to the British, Karam Singh informed the British of the whereabouts of the Jathedar and Sikh army.

Baba Ji and the Sikh soldiers were surrounded by the British and their Sikh cohorts, the Sikh Maharajah's' of

Patiala, Jind, Faridkot and other traitors along with the British army and their Patiala, Jind, Faridkot, Sikhs stooges opened up cannon fire on the Sikhs. 15,000 Sikhs attained martyrdom at the spot where the historic Gurdwara Dukh Niwaran of the ninth Sikh Guru, now stands in the city of Patiala. Budha Dal oral tradition states that 32,000 Singhs became shaheed during this battle.

Leader of the Sikh army, Jathedar Baba Hanuman Singh Ji and around 500 Nihang warriors survived this attack, and continued to fight the heavy cannon fire of the British, with swords, bows and arrows, axes and matchlock fire.

Finally after running out of gun powder and watching thousands of Sikh warriors achieve shaheedi, the brave Jathedar of the Guru's beloved Khalsa, Akaali Baba Hanuman Singh Ji died fighting for the freedom of the people of Punjab at the age of 90, in 1845.

After the martyrdom of Baba Hanuman Singh, Akaali Baba Prehlada Singh Ji became the 8th leader of the Akaali Nihang Singh Khalsa. The British implemented a shoot to kill order on the Nihang Singhs, and Baba Prehlada Singh left for the holy Takht Sahib at Nander to regroup the Akaali army. The few remaining Nihang Singhs, left with Baba Ji towards Hazoor Sahib, or moved camp to the jungles of Punjab and Rajputana to preserve the heritage of the Guru's army.

Gurdwara Sohana Sahib Ji located in the Mohali district of Punjab, was built on the shaheedi asthan (place of martrydom) of Baba Hanuman Singh Ji, in memory of a brave leader of the Sikh nation.

Baba Ji lived the life of a true Khalsa, and embodied the teachings of Sri Guru Granth Sahib Ji.

Akali Baba Hanuman Singh

Gurudwara Sohana Sahib (Mohali)